Forgive Me, Lord, I Goofed!

D0810801

Forgive Me, Lord, I Goofed!

Terry Helwig

BROADMAN PRESS
Nashville, Tennessee

Unless otherwise noted, Scripture quotations are from *The Living Bible.* Copyright ©
Tyndale House Publishers, Wheaton, Illinois, 1971. Used by permission.

Scripture quotations marked (KJV) are from the King James Version of the Bible.

Library of Congress Cataloging-in-Publication Data

Helwig, Terry, 1949-
  Forgive me, Lord, I goofed!

  1. Christian life—Baptist authors.   2. Forgiveness—
Religious aspects—Christianity. I. Title.
BV4501.2.H36956   1986   248.4'861   86-12887
ISBN 0-8054-5035-1

**With love to Jim and Mandy
and to God, the Father**

Acknowledgments: Denise George and Helen Parker

"Forgiveness is the fragrance the violet sheds on the heel that crushed it."

Preface

God's mirror of truth often finds me bare in my humanity. Many of my lessons of love and compassion have come at the most awkward, unflattering times in my life.

One sage commented that life is peculiar: it waits until we flunk the course to teach us a lesson.

I have discovered that statement to be true. I have learned painfully, and sometimes humorously, that no immunity exists from our human imperfections here on earth.

But I have not lost hope. There is a never-failing Cure.

The Lord!

Contents

My Very Human Condition

"It is the weak who are cruel. Gentleness can only be expected from the strong."—Rosten

The Grafting of Love

When I was twelve, my cousin Nancy, the same age as me, came to live with us. She expanded our family of seven to eight. Daddy then had seven females to contend with.

Our three-bedroom house absorbed Nancy without much rearranging. Someone gave up a drawer, a few more hangers wedged their way into our closet, and one more bed was shared. The emotional adjustments provided more of a challenge than the physical ones.

New routines had to be adopted and new needs met. We needed to love Nancy and she, us. We needed to accept her as a rightful heir to hugs, praises, and shared secrets. She needed a crash course in our family history.

She was not aware of our family "gremlins" that came in the night and mysteriously did away with the combs, brushes, and various toys that none of us had ever last used or seen. She did not know that "water otter eater" meant hot-water heater, so named because of my inability to pronounce that tongue twister until I was in the fourth grade. She wondered why my sister Vicki was called "me too," why the word *lipstick* brought laughter to everyone but Pattie, why Brenda was almost named Belinda, and how "Freckles" saved Joanne from a tarantula.

Telling Nancy these secrets did not produce instant results. Acceptance did not come in a week or even a month; fruitful grafting requires time. Our love could not be force bloomed; a gradual unfolding of days and experiences were required to move our hearts to love.

I knew why Nancy had come to live with us. Her mother, my aunt, drank too much and was no longer able to care for her properly. Mama said Nancy spent more time with baby-sitters than she did with her own mother, and Mama did not believe the sitters had Nancy's best interest at heart.

I knew all of that the afternoon Nancy and I stood on the porch. We were dividing up the folded, wet balls of clothes in the ironing basket. I was moving some of Daddy's shirts into her pile.

"I'm not going to iron any shirts," she informed me.

Her haughty reply irritated me. After all, I had family seniority over her.

"You better," I replied. "Or I'll inform Mama that you're not doing your share around here." I put my hand across the ironing board.

She had to stop ironing or the iron would burn my arm. "You can tell her anything you want, but I'm not ironing shirts," she snarled. "I didn't even have to iron when I lived with my mom."

"Well, we all work around here and pull our own weight. So if you want to stay here, you had better learn that."

"Who says I want to stay?" she asked. "Now move your arm!"

"And what if I don't?"

"Then I guess you'll get burned."

More was at stake than getting burned. A power struggle was underway, and I had no intention of losing. My hand stayed on the board.

"OK," she said. "Have it your way." She took a deep breath and pushed the iron into my flesh.

I screamed in pain and disbelief. She had taken the dare.

"You're terrible," I cried. "But what should I expect from someone whose mother is an alcoholic!"

Nancy sank to the floor sobbing. I had won. But the cost was too great, even for me. She had burned my flesh, but I had ripped out her heart.

For the first time, I realized the pain she felt being separated from her mom. It was not a separation she had asked for but one that had been deemed "the best for all concerned." She loved her mother as much as I loved mine. And she undoubtedly hated the amber bottles that robbed her of a love and relationship that most children never had to cry for.

I bent down beside her. "Nancy, I'm so sorry. That was a terrible thing to say. Can you ever forgive me?"

She looked up through tear-filled eyes. She put

her arms around me, and then we both cried. The grafting was complete; the flower of love had bloomed.

To this day, Nancy chooses to remember only the good from our years together. She forgives that twelve-year-old me standing on the back porch. God forgives me. And I guess, after all these years, it is time to forgive myself.

Nearsighted

I shivered inside my wool coat, retreating from the gray world into the solace of my own thoughts. Why wasn't the world warm, friendly, and summery instead of cold, unfriendly, and wintery? Where was my beloved sunshine, beaming like God's smile upon all the earth? Where was warmth and joy?

My spirit lay dormant within me, waiting. I longed for blue, sunny skies to thaw the thoughts of love and thanksgiving frozen within me. I longed for fragrant summer nights and . . .

"Mommy," my daughter Mandy's disgusted voice sounded from the back seat. Her impatience told me she must have tried repeatedly to penetrate my thoughts. I rewarded her efforts with my full attention.

"What, Sweetie?"

"Mommy? Isn't it just a beautiful day outside?"

Her comment jolted my sense of logic. Sleet scratched against the windshield, and the wind shoved the car at intermittent intervals. All around us—nothing but slush and barrenness.

I looked in the rearview mirror. Mandy's eyes glistened as she leaned forward in her car seat, looking out the window. She held her doll securely in her lap and waited for my reply.

Mandy's words stumbled through my mind. If they had fallen from any other lips, I would have laughed or made a sarcastic remark.

But out of my daughter comes pearl-sized bits of wisdom. Out of her comes a mirror that reflects a world much different from my own. Out of her comes a comment from a mind that has not yet been programmed to think that rain and sleet are unbeautiful.

When did my world change? In my childhood world, I splashed in rain puddles. And how many rainbows stretched across the sky as I ate warm fudge with my sister on the stoop of a rain-drenched porch? Snow crunched beneath me as I made angel wings. I sank in my grandma's feather bed and listened to sleet beat a melody on the attic roof.

I remember winter nights when embers glowed inside and snow flakes fell outside. I remember the morning I awoke to a glass forest. The crystal trees glistened in the sunlight. They bowed before me, their goblet-stemmed arms outstretched.

Nature took me by the hand and led me into the glass forest. My six-year-old mind stirred. Who created the magnificence before me? When a drop of water fell on my head, I looked upward and knew the answer.

Not one adult shared that moment with me. I was confused that evening as the grown ups mumbled to one another about treacherous ice storms, terrible roads, and power outages. Not one of them had traced their fingers over a cool, glassy branch. Not one of them had felt the fingertip of God drip upon their heads.

That memory wiped clean the film from my eyes. I looked out again at the gray, cotton-ball day. It was a day made for crackling fires, snuggles, and thanksgiving.

"Mommy," Mandy said again, waiting for an answer. "Isn't it beautiful?"

"Yes," I said as I looked upward. "Yes, yes, yes."

The Dinner Party

Jim and I wanted everything to be perfect because the couple coming for dinner were master entertainers. Their dinner parties rivaled the art and elegance of even the finest five-star restaurants. Their credits included brunches beside the rose garden and formal sit-down dinners for sixteen.

At one of their parties, we had seen our reflection in their antique dining-room table and admired a floral arrangement that almost touched their Venetian crystal chandelier. We had used Italian linens to blot paté from our mouths, drank water from English goblets, and ate from platters purchased in Portugal.

How would things work out? My linens came from the local department store; my menu called for charcoal-broiled; my plates had never been outside the United States. And then there was the question of what to do with our three-year-old daughter, Mandy. We certainly wanted to include her.

"I think it's a wonderful idea," Jim encouraged.

"Don't worry so much. I'll help you do every-thing."

So, we spent the day cleaning, cooking, setting the table for five, and mentally organizing the evening. Everything seemed to be unfolding beautifully.

That evening Mandy raced into the kitchen out of breath. "They're here. They're here. And the lady's got some flowers."

I accepted the basket of dewy, fragrant roses from Mrs. H. She had cut them that afternoon from her rose garden. "Thank you. They're just beautiful," I gushed. "I think we'll put them on the table."

After polite conversation, Jim excused himself. He was in charge of grilling the steaks. Even the rain did not deter him. He merely rolled the grill inside the garage and kept a watchful eye on the meat.

Meanwhile, I left Mandy to entertain our dinner guests while I finished making the salad and rice. As I lifted the lid off the rice, I complimented myself on how fluffy it had turned out. But the smug smile on my face disappeared when shrill, piercing alarms blasted through the stillness.

Thinking it was our security system, I ran to disarm it. But its green light stared serenely back at me, assuring me that all was well—with the security system anyway.

Just then Jim came running in. "I never knew the builder put a smoke alarm in the garage. How do you shut those things off?"

"I don't know. Unhook it maybe?"

"I can't believe it," he almost yelled. "All the alarms are going off—even the ones upstairs. They must be on the same circuit."

By that time, Mandy was screaming in the living room. Sirens terrify her. I ran to rescue her and tripped over our two cats in the dining room. They spun around and hissed, as though they had been attacked by a pack of siren-screeching wild dogs. Two patches of fur blurred past me. I turned the corner. There went Mandy on hands and knees up the stairs. She was headed in the direction of her security blanket. Mr. and Mrs. H. followed in hot pursuit.

Mandy fought them off. She probably remembered my beware-of-strangers-speech delivered just the past week. So, fleeing for her life, she kept screaming, "No. Get away from me. I want my Mommy and Daddy. Get away."

Finally, the alarms fell silent. Mandy stopped crying, but she would not let go of me. I held her while I watched Jim from the window. He stood beneath an umbrella while the grill hissed and sputtered in the rain. The cats slumped into the kitchen trying to figure out if they were safe. Any quick movement sent them into another tailspin. Things were not going as I had planned.

When we eventually sat down to dinner, Jim and I exchanged sympathetic glances. He shrugged his shoulders which made me smile. My eyes fell again on the roses, still wet with dew. They reminded me of a story I once read about two people. One was grieved by thorns while the other rejoiced over roses.

As Mandy pressed against me in the candle-light, I looked out at the table. I had so much for which to be thankful. My roses were many—my husband, my daughter, and our friends. But, still, my pride stung from the evening's events, and I found myself grieving over the thorns. Thorns that tried to keep me away from the roses. I did not want to be a thorn-griever. No, I wanted to rejoice.

So, carefully, I slid my hand into the evening and closed my fingers around a rose.

Closet Christian

At a luncheon, a guest speaker shared a turning point in her life with those of us in the audience.

She said her husband was a lawyer; she lived in a middle-class neighborhood. From the outside, she had appeared as the happy wife and mother of two children.

On the inside, however, she spent her days drinking from Vodka bottles hidden in the basement and laundry room. She was a closet alcoholic!

Her life lost focus, becoming a blur of half-remembered conversations. Her children, confused and hurt, retreated into their separate shells. Her husband, tired of searching and throwing out partially filled vodka bottles, asked for a divorce.

She looked out at us and said with tears in her eyes: "I don't know where all you Christians were, but no one ever told me before that God loved me—not until my neighbor invited me over for coffee one morning.

"It was there at her kitchen table, she took my

hand and said: 'I just want you to know that Jesus loves you right now, exactly as you are.'

"You cannot imagine what those words meant to me. I did not even love myself."

She said she went home and did something she had never done before—she prayed. There on her knees, her darkness vanished. There on her knees she found new life and for the first time in many years, she made contact with the good and worthy part of herself. She no longer needed vodka to make it through her days.

"That prayer," she said, "was made five years ago today."

As she sat down, her words echoed in my mind, especially the comment: "I don't know where all you Christians were, but no one ever told me before that God loved me."

Where had I been? Probably doing "my own thing," minding my own business, making sure not to offend anyone with my religious beliefs.

I believe in God and prayer. But I do not want someone to mistake me for a fanatic. I do not want to crawl out on a limb and run the risk of falling off.

The more I rationalized, the more I realized that I was a closet Christian, too embarrassed to talk about God. Not because I did not love Him but because I was not sure how my listeners might react.

I thought about Peter denying Christ three times that night long ago in Jerusalem. I won-

dered how many times I, too, had denied Him
with my silence.

"You forgave Peter, Lord. Please forgive me
too. What is it that makes me reluctant to reveal
my love for You?

"Help me to open my closet door and stick my
head out. Help me to speak or at least whisper."

The Words Never Came

My sister called and reported that Grandpa's doctors did not expect him to live much longer. They had found cancer, and it was spreading rapidly. I felt a need to hug his neck one last time, so I caught a plane the next day.

It was my first time back in three years. Grandma and Grandpa had since moved from the farm into a nursing home.

My footsteps echoed down the hall as I looked for their room. I passed a lady leaning to one side in her wheelchair. It looked to be an awkward position, but she smiled at me. Another woman reached for my hand.

"Help me," she pleaded. "Push me down there." She motioned obscurely in front of her. Wanting to help her, I wheeled her into what looked like a game room.

"Do you want to stay here?" I asked.

Her bottom lip started to tremble, and her eyes filled with tears: "No, not by myself."

I pushed her back to the nurse's station and asked the nurse to help me.

"Oh, she does that all the time," explained the nurse. "She'll have you pushing her everywhere. Just leave her."

Reluctantly, I walked away.

Grandma and Grandpa were glad to see me. Grandma liked the butterfly pin I gave her. She wanted me to put it on her right away.

Grandpa took the bow off his present and stuck it on top of his head. My other sisters were there, and they laughed, too. It almost seemed like the old days when Grandpa was strong and well and invincible.

He unwrapped the pillow that read: "Grand-children are the treasure of a long life." And he read aloud my note: "And you, Grandpa, are a treasure of the Lord. I shall always thank Him for making me part of your family."

"That's what it's all about," he said. His eyes fought to hold back tears.

We passed around the candy and cookies, looked at pictures, and talked about the great-grandchildren.

"Time goes so fast," Grandpa reflected. "Not in here, though. Sometimes it just seems to stand still. I took care of my mama for twenty years," he said. "We didn't have nursing homes then. But people do things differently these days." His words were not bitter, only wistful.

I wanted to hug him—this man who showed me how to put my hand under a hen and retrieve a warm, brown egg from her nest—this man who squirted milk at me as he squeezed the cow's udder—this man whose rough hands covered mine on the steering wheel of an old red tractor that carried us across summer fields.

How I wanted to say, "Come live with me, Grandpa. I'll fix up the spare bedroom for you and Grandma. I'll hang bright, white curtains, just like the ones that used to dance in the evening breezes blowing across the farm.

"We'll plant a garden and fill our arms with sun-warmed tomatoes and squash. We'll sit in the glider and listen to the doves coo in the morning and the crickets chirp at night.

"My daughter can crawl up into your lap as love bridges the span of years between the two of you. And by the end of summer, when her dresses have grown too short, we can shake our heads and sigh, 'My, my! Where has all the time gone?' "

I wanted to ask you to come live with me, Grandpa. But the words never came. . . . I guess I was afraid you might say yes.

Kites
and Knights-in-Shining Armor

I heard the pad-pad of my three-year-old's footsteps. I checked my watch. It confirmed my suspicions. An hour had somehow passed. Rest time was over.

"Can we fly the kite now?" She wanted to know.

I did not want to. I had so much to do. But Mandy looked like a puppy waiting for his ball to be thrown. How could I say no? I closed the door to my office and made a silent promise to return that night.

There is a certain excitement associated with trying to elevate a kite into the air. An anticipation. A feeling of elation as the wind snaps the plastic and pulls it away from you.

The twine unraveling in the palm of your hand casts a magical spell. Children stop their play. They come like the Wise Men following a star. They stare into the spring sky and seem to share your victory—that part of yourself that flies with the kite.

I wish I could say that is how our afternoon of kite flying went. But our experience was not quite so poetic. The kite stubbornly refused to fly. It trailed behind me flapping, fluttering, and dive-bombing the vacant lot.

"Thwack!" It hit the ground for the sixth time.

"I'll get it," Mandy volunteered as she caught her foot in the twine. Like a netted animal, she screeched, twisted, and turned. By the time I reached her, she looked like a package tied for mailing.

Our neighbor Brett appeared on the scene. He offered his help. He got Mandy untied but could do little for the mass of tangled string and twigs. So, we cut the string and started over. He held up the kite, and I ran once more.

The kite looped and surged upward. The string unraveled with fishing-reel precision.

"Hurray."

Our kite was airborne.

"Don't let it blow away," Mandy warned.

"Don't worry, Honey. See this string." I held up the ball of twine to show her. Unaware that my credibility was at stake, the kite yanked the last of the string from my hand and headed east.

"Oh no," I yelled.

"I'll get it," Brett reassured. And off he went, chasing a kite that never intended to be captured again.

The kite turned into a speck in the distance followed by an innocent, earthbound, little boy. I did not know who to feel sorrier for—Mandy or Brett.

"Will Brett bring back my kite?"

"I don't think so, Honey. I'm very sorry. I'll buy you another kite tomorrow. Okay?"

"Maybe Brett will find it," Mandy said more for her benefit than mine.

I did not think so . . . until I saw an orange shape moving in the distance. Could it be?

Brett, like a knight-in-shining-armor, grinned and waved. He raised the kite over his head in a victory salute.

"He found it! He found it!" Mandy ran to greet him.

"It was hung up in a tree," Brett reported.

His face was flushed from running. Out of breath, he handed me the wounded kite.

"I wanted so much to get it for her. I know what it's like to lose a kite."

"Thank you," I replied sincerely. "I never thought you'd catch up with it."

We walked back to the house, and I looked over at the two of them—my daughter and her "knight." She marched beside him, her eyes full of gratitude. He met her gaze with a smile, and the two of them stepped into their shared moment of understanding—a place unfamiliar to me.

Conditioned to live in a world of wars and famines and earthquakes, I had forgotten the simpler moments of childhood. Flying kites and finding kites—those were the kind of moments I might be tempted to sweep under a rug. "I'm too busy," I might argue. "Forget the crumbs. Give me a whole slice of life to enjoy—vacations, parties, holidays, weekends."

But children know better. They love crumbs—those little morsels of living that are sweet and satisfying on the tongue. They love the way raindrops freckle sidewalks. They have time to watch a worm inch its way across a twig, and some even have the courage and wisdom to chase a small friend's kite.

Three Extra Days

I sat down in front of the television set and flipped on the remote control. After running through the five channels, I could not find anything that looked very good, so I settled for a detective show. I soon was caught up in the plot.

A woman had been kidnapped. Two men had already been shot and dumped into the ocean after attempting to save her. The detective rented a boat and went undercover as a drug smuggler. Luckily, his cover was not blown until the very end. He managed to save the woman, and justice was served when the boat and helicopter blew up, killing the "bad guys." The woman put her arms around the detective, and they drove into the sunset.

After the show, I planned on writing a few letters, doing my ironing and mending, and polishing my fingernails, but I soon became interested in the movie that followed. I forgot about my little list of chores. When I remembered them that night before going to bed, I told myself: *Oh, well. Tomorrow is another day.*

The next afternoon, I tuned in to see what was happening on my daytime serial. Tom definitely wanted a divorce from Erica after he found out she had been lying about trying to have a baby; Wally learned of Devon's affair; and Carrie gave Tad some marijuana. And I had to tune in the next day because Cliff, no doubt, was going to discover that Nina did not want to marry him because she thought she was going blind.

I still needed to write those letters, iron, mend, and paint my fingernails, but Mandy was up from her nap and wanted some attention.

I can probably do those things tonight, while I watch television, I rationalized.

So my days and nights went for more than a year after my daughter was born. I did not realize I had become addicted to my daily doses of television until I read an article on the subject. The article quoted Marie Winn who wrote *The Plug-In Drug.*

Ms. Winn suggested that television viewing allowed a person to blot out the real world and enter into a pleasurable and passive mental state—much like the "high" induced by drugs or alcohol. And like alcoholics who believe they can control their drinking, Ms. Winn wrote that many people overestimate their control over television.

"Even as they put off other activities to spend

hour after hour watching television, they feel they could easily resume living in a different, less passive style. But somehow or other, while the television set is present in their homes, the click doesn't sound."[1]

I thought long and hard about my television habits. Did I watch a program because I really wanted to? Not always. Sometimes I did not even like what was on, but sitting in the family room with the television off was like sitting in the dark without a light.

After looking through the television guide, I discovered only a handful of programs that really interested me. What a revelation! I also discovered I could add three working days to my schedule by cutting out television. Three extra days!

I decided to reform. I did not go so far as my friend who took the scissors and cut the cord to her television, but I did force myself to click off the set or remove myself from the room while my husband watched something I was not interested in.

At first, I felt displaced—lonely, at a loss as what to do with myself. I realized I was, indeed, suffering from withdrawal. I prayerfully asked God what He wanted me to do with my three extra days. It did not take Him long to answer.

"Ever since you were a little girl you wanted to write. Remember the 'book' you wrote when you were nine? Well, follow that dream: the one you said you never had time for. And while you're at it . . . put in a good word for Me!"

1. Marie Winn, *The Plug-In Drug* (New York: Viking Penguin, 1985), p. 24.

None Today

What should I do with the "leftover" leftover meat loaf? Eating it three times in one week seemed enough to me, so I stuffed the rest of it down the garbage disposal.

I turned my attention to the refrigerator. As I rummaged through the shelves, I came upon an unopened carton of sour cream—the expiration date long before reached. I admonished myself as I plopped white, heaping tablespoons into the disposal.

So it went as I cleaned out the refrigerator. The limp celery went into the trash. The moldy piece of cheese, leftover hamburger patty, and cup of mashed potatoes joined the meat loaf and sour cream.

Then with a flick of my finger, I turned on the disposal and ground up all the food. Presto! No more garbage! I turned out the lights on my clean kitchen and clean refrigerator.

Meanwhile, another mother halfway around the world, sat on the barren earth in Ethiopia. With hopeful eyes, she watched a doctor walk through the crowds. *Maybe today,* she thought. *Maybe today, he will give us food.*

She held up her frail child for the doctor to see. The doctor looked at her and sadly shook his head no. Gently he told her there was not enough food for her child today.

The doctor had to choose which people would be fed and which would not. His dilemma: There was not enough food to feed everyone in the large crowds gathered outside the center. He tried to determine who would die that day without food. Who could wait until the next?

The mother drew her child near her. Desperation filled her eyes. She would have to wait yet another day.

A woman beside her cried out in sorrow. She crawled in the dust and covered her face with her hands. A small bundle lay at her feet. Her baby had just died.

How I wish these stories were not true, but they are! Liz Kliewer, a teenager who visited Ethiopia, saw these things with her own eyes. She held the hands and cried with the mother whose child died. She saw the pain written on the other mother's face when the doctor shook his head no and said no food today.[1]

I have a three-year-old daughter. She is healthy; she leaves food on her plate; she plays with her toys and splashes in her bath water every night. I cannot even imagine the agony of the mother who watches as her child dies gradually from starvation and disease.

What would those mothers think of little gadgets invented to grind up excess food and garbage? What would they think of a woman who throws away food because she does not want to eat the same stuff four times in one week? What would they think of a nation that destroys food in order to keep the marketplace from being glutted?

Those questions overwhelmed me. What was I supposed to do? There were so many homeless, so many hungry, so many dying. Surely my efforts were like trying to clear away an avalanche of human suffering with a teaspoon.

But I realized the danger in that type of thinking—a heart waxing cold, the seeds of apathy being sown. So I got out my teaspoon—a pen—and started to dig. I pledged to send a check every month to a nonprofit organization that attempts to feed the world's hungry.

What do I hope to accomplish? Maybe nothing more than providing one more bowl of rice. But to the mother who raises her child for the doctor to see, it will be enough.

1. Liz Kliewer, "Through the Eyes of A Teenage Christian," *World Vision*, April-May 1985, pp. 7-8.

Too Little, But Not Too Late

"A man wrapped up in himself makes a very small bundle."

The Sour Grape

If only there were two of me, I thought, *maybe then I could answer yes to all the caring, conscientious people who are asking for my help in worthwhile projects.*

I tried to say yes when I could. Yes, I would furnish cookies for my daughter's school party. Yes, I could drive the youth club on Sunday. Yes, I would be honored to be a leader at church. Yes, I would find the necessary time to go to the meetings and work on the committees. Yes, the United Way was a worthwhile organization. Yes, I realized the wives at my husband's office regularly volunteered to solicit funds. Yes, I would be willing to help them out again this year.

My yeses left fewer and fewer minutes. Stringing together enough time to write was already a problem. If I wanted to continue with my writing ministry, I realized I would have to start saying no, no matter how worthy the cause.

A day after my decision, the phone rang.

"Hi, this is Sally. I met you several months ago at Sue's."

"Oh, yes," I answered. "You and your husband live a few blocks from here?"

"That's right," she replied. "Listen, I don't know if you're familiar with Crime Watch. But I'm the regional director . . ."

My instincts told me to watch out. I mentally ran through a list of reasons for saying no to what was about to be asked. *Remain calm,* my inner voice directed. *Say it is impossible for you to take on any more responsibility at this time. Remember the book you're working on.*

Right, I said to myself. *Remember the book.*

"So, I was wondering," Sally continued, "if you would be block captain?"

My inner voice nudged me. *Go on. Tell her you can't possibly do it.*

I followed the suggestion. "I'm afraid I just can't take on any more than what I'm doing now. I'm involved at school and at church, and I'm also a writer."

I felt quite proud of myself. I actually said no. I lowered my defenses. Sally started with the counterattack. I was unprepared.

"There's really not that much to do. I'm busy, too, you know, but this is a worthwhile project. And it's for our own neighborhood. I really don't know anyone else on your block I can call."

I stammered for a moment. "Are there any meetings involved? I can't commit to any more nightly meetings."

"No, there are hardly any meetings—maybe once a year."

The only thing left to say seemed to be yes. I did not say it with feeling or warmth or pleasure. I said it with about as much enthusiasm as two children who are forced to apologize after a fight. Angry feelings churned inside me. I did not know who to direct them toward, Sally or myself.

When Sally called the next day to tell me there was a meeting the following evening, I could not help but act aloof and cold. After all, I specifically asked if there would be meetings involved. Even her offer to pick me up did little to melt the ice cube inside me.

When she came to the door that evening, I politely thanked her for the ride. When she thanked me for agreeing to be block captain, I could think of nothing positive to say, so I remained silent. When she apologized for the fact that a meeting had been scheduled so soon, I let her know I was surprised also. When she asked me what kind of writing I did, the word *Christian* stuck in my throat.

I felt embarrassed. My declaration obviously surprised Sally, and I knew why. How could she have guessed that the lady who grudgingly rode beside her in the car wrote about forgiveness and love? How could an ice cube radiate God's warmth? How could God's sweet message of grace come from such a sour grape?

One of Paul's messages came to mind. "Let him give; not grudgingly, or of necessity: for God loveth a cheerful giver" (2 Cor. 9:7, KJV).

Sally drove a changed woman home from the

meeting that night: one who had learned something about giving, one who had learned that if she said yes, God wanted it to come from her heart, not merely her lips!

Sunday Stew

Churning with hurt and angry feelings, I drove to church. The thought of my husband—pouring himself a glass of orange juice and casually flipping through the Sunday paper—made me simmer.

At least he knew how I felt. Even though I did not verbalize anything, my monotone voice and cool manner surely revealed my true feelings.

Upon arriving in Sunday school, I felt worse. I was one of the few people without a mate. *How do these women get their husbands to come?* I wondered. I studied the three husbands who came without their wives. What motivated them to come by themselves?

After class one of the men came over to me. "Does your husband ever come to class with you?"

"No. I just can't seem to get him here," I admitted.

"I know what you mean," he replied. "I'm trying to get my wife to come too. We'll just have to pray about it, won't we?"

The man's suggestion clanged like a bell. Pray about it. Why hadn't I thought of that?

"I see your husband in church," he added. "That's good."

Then as luck would have it—no, I should say, as God would have it—I sat right behind that man in the sanctuary. Before the service began, I heard him ask his daughter if she had seen her mother yet. She shrugged her shoulders and shook her head to signify no.

As we bowed our heads to pray, his wife slipped into the pew beside him. He smiled and winked at her. Tenderly, he took her hand and held it during the prayer.

Two hours at church and my whole situation turned on me.

Of the two souls God saw that morning, which was the more pleasing? The one praying that his wife would join him? Or the one in the pew behind him—stewing because her husband didn't?

The answer was obvious: stewing is for soups, not Christians!

Unplanted Seed

How do you ease the pain of a woman whose six-month-old granddaughter lies in "serious condition"?

"Child abuse"—that's what the report indicated.

How do you help her cope with the heart-wrenching news that her own daughter has been charged with negligence in the horrible act? What words can put to rest the doubt in her mind as her daughter cries, "I didn't do it, Mom. Please believe me."

"I'll pray for you" seemed to be all I could think of. So I wrote those words in my letter. Somehow, I hoped they would help ease her pain and give her comfort.

I mailed the letter and went through my myriad chores and errands. At the dinner table that night, Jim and I discussed the situation again.

"The poor baby," he said. "Children are so vulnerable. Completely defenseless. You wonder how anyone could possibly harm them."

"Let's pray for them," I suggested. "Let's pray

that somehow God will be able to squeeze some goodness from the situation. Let's pray that He heals the baby's broken spirit, as well as her body."

But before we could pray, the phone rang. I talked for awhile, then cleared away the dinner dishes, and sorted the laundry. I gave my daughter a bath, read to her, and tucked her securely into bed. As I bent to kiss her, I thought of the baby in the hospital. How confused and frightened she must feel.

"Dear Lord . . ." I began.

"Terry, can you come here for a minute?" Jim called. I went downstairs, forgetting about my unfinished prayer. My husband and I talked and watched television until bedtime.

Once in bed, I suddenly remembered I had to go to the dentist the next day. I had forgotten all about it. That meant I would have to switch the baby-sitter from Tuesday to Monday, work on my article Wednesday, and drive my daughter to the library on Thursday. By the time I had mentally arrived at Friday, I had fallen asleep. No prayers. No listening. No remembering.

My empty words, "I'll pray for you," lay like unplanted seed in the palm of my hand.

I once heard the expression, "Satan laughs at our toiling, mocks at our wisdom, but trembles when we pray."

How sad that Satan had nothing to fear from me that night. How tragic that the power of my prayers lay unleashed within me. How heartbreaking that I missed an opportunity to cradle a battered child and touch the heart of an aching grandmother. How terribly pathetic that I left undone the most important service I could have done for them—or for any human being. For what can be more life changing than lifting a broken spirit into the healing light of prayer?

Ignorance Is No Excuse

"Do you ladies want to play a tie breaker or a third set?"

"A third set," I said.

"A tie breaker," my partner, Betty, suggested simultaneously.

I shifted my racket to the other hand and shot a disapproving look at her. Didn't she realize how important this match was to the team? The rules stated that if players had more than twenty minutes left, they should begin a third set. According to the clock, we still had twenty-three minutes.

"I think we should begin the third set," I advised emphatically.

Betty looked at me with a pained expression on her face. "OK," she sighed and walked back to the forehand side. Her behavior irritated me.

Why was she annoyed? She was the reason for the discussion in the first place. If she had been on time, we would have had plenty of time to play. I was the one who should be tired; I warmed up with our opponents for fifteen minutes before she arrived.

I didn't want to be angry with her, but every time she missed a shot I found myself bristling. She wasn't hustling or lining up for the shot. Obviously she cared little about the outcome of the game. I only hoped I didn't have to play with her every week.

As we walked off the court, our opponents hurried to the desk to report their victory. They won the third set in fifteen minutes—we didn't even win a game.

"I'm sorry," Betty apologized as we walked out.

"That's OK," I answered, trying to be friendly. *After all,* I told myself, *it was only a game.*

"The reason I didn't want to play a third set," she explained, "is because I've been having terrible headaches for several weeks now. I'm due to go to the hospital for tests."

"Why didn't you tell me you weren't feeling well?" I insisted. I at least wanted a chance to be charitable. "Did you try to get a sub to play for you today?"

"No. I just can't quit living."

Her reply confused me. What did getting a sub have to do with living? I chatted for a while longer, still somewhat irritated by the fact she hadn't told me she was feeling sick.

Several weeks later, I learned Betty was in the hospital for brain surgery. They operated and found a tumor. A surprise to me, but probably not to her, because I also learned she had been battling cancer, in one form or another, for the past five years.

That's what she meant when she answered, "I can't quit living."

How many days had she tried to struggle through her pain? I wondered. How many people had she encountered, like me, who didn't make allowances for her courageous battle? How many times was the outcome of a tennis game more important than the fact this lady was out there trying to go on?

I was reminded of a story about a man who, when bumped, growled: "Watch where you're going, Mister!"

It turned out the mister was blind.

God cradled me in His arms that night. He knew I hurt.

"Forgive me, Lord, for the times I, too, have spoken harsh words in ignorance. Help me learn from this experience. Help me look beyond a situation, realizing that many times, maybe even most times, there are reasons why people say and do the things they do.

"Help me see what You see—confused, struggling children—some who are hurting, some who are lost, and some who have forgotten why they live."

To Love a Friend

Sue's death numbed me with disbelief. She was one of my best friends. We didn't call or write regularly, but then we didn't have to. We always managed to pick up our friendship right where we left it off—finishing each other's sentences and thoughts.

But then I talked to Eirin, one of Sue's other friends. She called to share her grief after hearing about Sue.

"I loved her so much," she said. "You know, I called her often. She always seemed to see the funny side of everything."

I, too, remembered the few calls Sue and I shared over the years. Old stories bloomed again; new stories were born. And if there were tears of gladness or sadness, they fell shamelessly on the shoulders at the other end of the silent receiver.

So why did Eirin's call disturb me so much? Was it because she remembered Sue's birthday and I had forgotten it? Was it because I remembered how often she wrote to Sue when Sue moved to Australia? Was it because she sent Sue chocolate chips to make her favorite cookies? Was it because she was the first one to visit Sue when she returned to the States—even though it meant going two hundred miles out of her way? Or was it because I had not taken advantage of all the times I, too, could have said, "I'm thinking about you"?

An unexpected note in the mailbox, words reaching out like a warm, loving hug—how many times had that small act changed my mood or brightened my day? And the time a friend sent me a prism to hang in my window. Perhaps it was a small gift to her, but to me . . . the beginning of mornings filled with rainbows, afternoons dancing with color, and days flowing with continuous thoughts of the beautiful person responsible!

Those are the little things that life is said to consist of. And, now, I find myself playing the "if-only . . ." game. *If only* I had given Sue a prism to hang in her window, . . .

Brothers and Sisters in Christ

On Easter morning, the notes of "Sweet Adoration" took wing inside a country church. They wrapped themselves around the white velvet lillies, touched the rustic cross draped with purple, and ascended to the topmost stained-glass window. A warm glow settled about the head and shoulders of the congregation.

Tears threatened to run down my cheeks and splash onto the floor. What would the others around me think? I opened my eyes wide and tried to choke back the emotion stirred by the song. But the words—exquisite and lilting—kept coming.

> When I am troubled, by heartache and struggle,
> I come and adore you,
> You take me away from
> all worldly sensation,
> and endless temptation;
> All of my trials are lost in Your love.[1]

The woman next to me sniffled and stopped singing. Her shoulders shook, and I saw her daughter's arm go around her. I, too, wanted to comfort her. I wanted to blurt out, "I know how you feel. Isn't this song beautiful? It's filled with such love and forgiveness. It makes me feel more like I am your sister rather than a stranger."

But those transcending words lay trapped within me, bound by social graces. No normal person hugs total strangers. How embarrassing! So the woman next to me never knew how I felt. I did not reach out.

Still I pray that someday I might meet that lady again as the lyrics of "Sweet Adoration" vibrate the heavens. I pray that we will not be strangers in physical bodies but two souls basking in the presence of God. And if I ever see her again, I want to confess: "Remember me? I stood beside you on earth one Easter morning. I wanted to hug you while you were crying, but I didn't know how."

---

1. Written by Lynn Sutter, Dawn Rodgers and Brown Bannister. Copyright © 1980 Bug and Bear Music. Exclusive adm. by LCS Music Group, Inc., P.O. Box 202406, Dallas, TX 75220. Int'l copyright secured. All rights reserved. Used by Permission.

The Rejection Slip

Three rejection slips in the same afternoon—that could prick even the toughest writer's hide.

You call yourself a writer, a voice taunted from within. *You spend hours up in that room, writing, rewriting, and not writing. Look where it gets you.*

I read the rejections. "Sorry, your manuscript does not meet our editorial needs at this time." "We regret that the enclosed manuscript does not fit into our publishing plans. Best wishes on further contributions." "Thank you for sending us this material. We have examined it carefully and found that it does not fulfill our present editorial requirements. We shall be glad to receive other contributions which you may think suitable."

"Editorial needs"—those innocuous words eroded my self-confidence.

Why had I given up shopping sprees, tennis, and lunches with my friends? Why did I put my daughter down for her nap and run to my keyboard instead of the television set? Why did I lie awake at night searching for exactly the right word or just the right phrase? Why?

The answers whispered in my ear. *You write because you cannot do otherwise. You write because you feel compelled to funnel your soul onto paper. You write because you want to convince others that what they so desperately cry out for is God's love. Never doubt your uniqueness. No one else can write what lies within you.*

The words of Og Mandino in his book *The Greatest Miracle in the World* came to my mind.

"Never, in all the seventy billion humans who have walked this planet since the beginning of time has there been anyone exactly like you.

"Never, until the end of time, will there be another such as you.

"You have shown no knowledge or appreciation of your uniqueness.

"Yet you are the rarest thing in the world."[1]

My discouragement and self-pity melted away. God had never sent me a rejection slip. "I'm sorry, but you do not fulfill My present editorial needs. Please try again in the future."

No, He always accepts me. I am unique, and I am His.

"Then what do you want me to do about these rejections?" I asked.

That's when I found myself seated in front of my word processor!

1. Og Mandino, *The Greatest Miracle in the World* (New York: Bantam, 1985), p. 97.

The Ministering Angel

I read an article about Trevor Ferrell. It seems that one December afternoon, after hearing a televised report about Philadelphia's street people, Trevor asked his parents to drive him downtown. He wanted to give away a pillow and one of his blankets.

Trevor was only eleven years old. Yet his parents went outside and started the car. They didn't pat him on the head and alibi, "That's very sweet, Trevor, but we can't go down there."

No, they must have listened to a wiser Voice—a Voice that said their son's faith could somehow change things. Because, change things it did.

That night, one of Philadelphia's street people slept under Trevor Ferrell's blanket. That night, unbeknown to Trevor, the compassion he felt would soon make him nationally famous.

Most evenings thereafter, Trevor and his family gathered food and blankets to take downtown. Neighbors heard about Trevor's efforts and started donating food and clothing. Churches heard. Newspapers and television stations ran

stories about the "Ministering Angel" of Philadelphia's street people.

The more publicity Trevor received, the more
people wanted to give—cash and checks, an
anonymously donated Volkswagen van to help
Trevor make his rounds, one hundred surplus
overcoats from an Army training center, and a
thirty-room house in the inner city to be used as
a shelter for the street people.

Trevor's one act of kindness snowballed into a
program that is now helping hundreds.

I lack Trevor Ferrell's insight. When my friend
and I came upon an unconscious man on the sidewalk in New York City, we bent over him.

"What can we do for him?" Sue asked helpless-
ly.

I looked at the empty wine bottle next to the
man. A trickle of purple stained the concrete.
"There isn't anything we can do, Sue." I pulled
Sue away. "It's sad, but even if we tried to help
him, he would probably end up here again tomorrow."

Perhaps Sue saw a glimpse of what Trevor saw.
She looked back. It truly saddened her to see a
human life crumpled upon the sidewalk like garbage.

"Come on," I urged. "We'll be late for the
play."

Probably a thousand people passed that man's
way that day.

Sometimes at night, I wonder what happened
to that man. Did a Trevor Ferrell come along? Did

he offer the man something to eat? Did a young
boy, who could see farther into the kingdom than
I, bend tenderly to touch that man's shoulder and
stroke his face?

Did he whisper into the man's ear, "It doesn't
matter that you might be here again tomorrow.
For today, know that I care. I give you my comfort, my love, and my blanket."

The Accident

I backed up to allow a lady in front of me room to pull into a parking space.

A horn blared and *crunch!* My car hit something. I looked back to my left. Another lady yelled at me through the closed windows of her car.

I wanted to lock my doors and curl into a fetal position, but I opened my door instead.

The other woman stood, sergeantlike, and spoke hotly.

"I just got this car three days ago. It's brand-new."

I guess I should have been more sympathetic to the fact that her car was new, but I was honest.

"I'm sorry, but I wouldn't have intentionally bumped into you no matter how old your car was."

She kept shaking her head and rubbing her car.

My bumper showed no signs of damage. She was not so fortunate. The area in front of her wheel folded into a good-sized dent which exposed ugly metal.

"You'd better go call the police," she snapped.

"OK," I got back into the car to move it out of the way.

Like a hawk swooping from the sky, she came at my car and pounded on the hood. "You can't move your car; the police won't write up an accident report if you move."

I could not believe how the scene was unfolding. I had driven twenty years without an accident. Maybe I should have been grateful, but the lady's ranting and raving in front of me made me feel anything but grateful.

Keep cool, I told myself. *Turn the other cheek and all that stuff.*

"I'm sorry," I apologized. "I've never been in an accident before. I didn't know."

"Will you just go call the police," she yelled.

My heart pounded, I felt like exploding, and tears threatened to break through. I found a phone and tried to steady my fingers in order to dial correctly.

"We'll have a car there in a few minutes," the dispatcher told me.

I went back outside. The woman waited in her car and I in mine.

Five minutes later an officer arrived. His manner calmed me as I explained how I had accidentally backed into the other car. He filled out an accident report and told us to get in touch with our insurance agencies.

The woman started crying.

I wanted to comfort her.

"I know it doesn't help," I consoled, "but I'm truly sorry."

"Three years from now, it probably won't make any difference," she came back, hostility still hissing in her voice. "Just watch where you're going from now on."

By the next evening, I was able to calm down a bit. I realized it was not the accident but the woman's reaction to it that bothered me so much. What did she think the word *accident* meant? Could she have been any more upset if I had deliberately run my car into hers? I did not think so.

The phone rang.

"Hi, this is B. J., the lady you ran into yesterday. I need to get in touch with your insurance agency, and I can't find them listed in the phone book. Do you have their number?"

"Just a minute," I answered coolly.

I located the number and got back on the phone. "What do you need the number for?" I asked.

"Because, Lady, I have to rent a car to go to work!"

I started to give her the number, but she interrupted.

"Why isn't it listed in the phone book? What kind of insurance is this anyway? Are you sure you even have insurance?"

"Listen," I told her. "I have taken just about as much abuse as I am going to take from you over this."

"You're taking abuse! What do you think I'm taking? I'm the one . . ."

I didn't hear what else she said because I hung up the phone.

It immediately rang again, and my husband answered. He gave her the phone number and told her our agents would take care of the details. She said she had no intention of calling her insurance company and hung up.

I was more upset than ever. How could a dented fender cause so much grief? Yet I knew it was not the dented fender but the hostility between this woman and me that kept me awake most of the night.

I tried to think what Jesus might do in a similar situation. Somehow, I did not think He would hang up the telephone as I had. He would not meet hostility with hostility. Instead, He would surely absorb it and try to turn it into a loving action.

I had already apologized. What else could I do? Short of going back in time and not running into her, I could think of nothing. A phone call did not seem to be the answer.

Why not send flowers? The question popped into my mind.

Flowers? What if she threw them into the garbage or something?

What if she did? the wiser part of me replied. *At least you would have made an attempt to soothe the situation.*

For some reason, it was very important to try and right the situation.

I walked into the florist shop and selected a spring bouquet: purple iris and yellow tulips waving from a woven basket.

"Do you want to sign a card?" the florist asked.

I searched for the right words.

"Dear B. J., Just my attempt to make peace . . . I'm sorry about the harsh words and hard feelings caused by the accident. I'm really not a bad person, and I suspect, neither are you. May God bless and keep you in His care. Terry H."

The heavy weight I had been carrying since the accident lifted.

What did B. J. do with the flowers? I'll probably never know. But maybe when she reflects on our accident, she won't be able to do so without also thinking of a spring bouquet . . . and neither will I.

Graffiti

A can of red paint had been used to spray words of hatred and disrespect. There was no escaping them—they hung like ugly pictures on the tile walls inside the tunnel. Even the subway cars did not escape. Graffiti, in black and red and blue, clashed against the beige paint above the doors and windows. As I bounced in my seat, I read the walls and wondered about those people who had autographed the world with their cans of spray paint.

Who were they? What motivated them? What made them hurt? What made them cry? What made them laugh?

As I asked myself the unanswerable questions, my eyes rested on a tiny flower painted above one of the doors. It was primitive, like a six-year-old's drawing—five awkward, uneven petals amid the graffiti. It looked out of place, like a pearl dropped onto a mound of coffee grounds. Its mark was not brutal like the others. It was imperfect and tender—an attempt to create beauty.

As I stared at the flower and the other graffiti

on the subway walls, I realized how often I myself
have gone through life with a case of spray paint.
I walk into someone's room, perhaps someone I
don't even know, and I spew words of anger and
insensitive remarks onto their walls. The waiter
who forgot to bring the bread and then the butter,
the service man who came an hour later than he
was supposed to, the insensitive clerk in the store
—I have sprayed, in bright red paint, my preju-
dices and judgments across the white enamel of
their lives. I have left my mark, my autograph, my
"Christian" graffiti on their walls.

Sometimes those closest to me get sprayed on
the most. They see me when I am tired and depressed, when I am at such loose ends that I pick
up my can of paint and aim at anything in sight.
I seldom mean what I write on their walls, but
paint is hard to scrub off. Even though I try to
wipe my remarks clean with apologies, some still
leave ugly shadows. And no matter how hard I try
to banish them, those shadows sometimes surface
on tender egos and budding self-esteem.

For that reason, I am more careful what I say
with my cans of spray paint. I try to draw flowers
now because flowers leave prettier shadows. And
even though my flowers are crude and primitive—
like a six-year-old's—they symbolize perfectly my
imperfect attempts to love others as myself.

A Psalm for Mama

At twenty-seven with six children at home, Mama went back to school for her high school diploma. After that, she spent late nights studying nursing manuals.

The nights the light shone beneath her bedroom door, the hours spent memorizing the name of every bone in the human body, the countless times she stuck a needle into an orange to practice giving shots—all of it paid off.

I remember when her name was called at graduation: Carola Jean Woytek. She rose and went forward. The stiff white hat on her head gave proof to the world that Mama had made it. She was a nurse.

And if the story ended on the night of her graduation—surely, we would have all lived happily ever after.

But it did not. Mama's hectic schedule soon proved too demanding. She started taking different medications. At first, she gave herself vitamin B-12 shots. Then she needed sleeping pills, and eventually bottles of sedatives and pain killers lined the top of her dresser. I found hypodermic needles and never wanted to know what had been in them.

All I wanted was a mother like the other kids had. One who filled the kitchen with the sweet smell of home-baked cookies. One who attended PTA meetings. One who washed the laundry on Mondays and grocery shopped on Tuesdays.

"I'm not the stereotyped mother you see in your mind," Mama told me. "I'm not ready to go through life with a shawl around my shoulders, sitting in some rocking chair."

Still, I sensed she wanted my approval.

"I was married and had you by the time I was fifteen," she often reminded me. "I didn't know how to cook, clean—not even how to iron. That's not going to happen to you girls. That's why I make you do everything."

"I'm sorry you had such a rough life, Mama. But why do we have to pay for it?"

Those words live on.

Mama did not. She died before her forty-first birthday. Before we ever had a chance to work things out between us. Before I myself became a mother.

But time and God are patient teachers to the living. And I have learned much in their class-room. They took my mother's favorite book in the Bible—the Psalms—and unveiled her fears, her pain, her weaknesses and, most importantly, her strengths.

God and time helped me focus on the positive. They helped me recall Mama's many shining moments: the time she made a meal for a ragged beggar, the times she lifted my tear-streaked face to her own, the time she handed a package to my cousin who had come to live with us.

"See," Mama told my cousin as she squeezed her shoulders. "I told you your mother wouldn't forget about you." Not even Mama knew I had seen her buy and wrap that very package.

How had I overlooked all the shining moments? How much pain had I caused with my looks of disapproval, my looks that accused, my looks that sneered: Woman, you are not the mother of my dreams.

That is why I write just one more psalm—for you, Mama.

Forgive me for the times I may have hurt you. Hear the song of love in my heart.

I do not remember the times I drank from your breasts, or the times I slept in your arms, or the times you sat beside me as I tossed with fevers.

I do not remember them, but I know those times existed. I have experienced those times with my daughter who will also not remember them.

I now understand things only mothers understand.

And at night, when I bend over and kiss your granddaughter, I sometimes feel your love in the room.

I only hope . . . you can feel mine too!

Granny's Circle

My husband narrowed his brow in my direction. Without words he made it plain, "How did I ever let you talk me into this?"

I wondered the same thing. The tight circle of chairs flashed a warning light in my mind. Group therapy! Evidently the marriage-enrichment weekend required group interaction as well as couple interaction.

I suspected the other three couples, seated in the small room with us, shared our dilemma. To look anywhere but down meant an encounter with someone else's eyes. So the six of us deployed creative behaviors to avoid eye contact.

One woman studied her wedding rings as if seeing them for the first time. The older gentleman across from me picked lint off his trousers. My husband stared at his watch as though he could not figure out the time. And I suddenly became fascinated with my shoes.

The moderator was overly cheerful. "Let's go around the circle and tell everyone a little bit about ourselves," she bubbled.

Our introductions were formal and stiff. *Never a more unlikely group to be paired together,* said the little judge that lives inside me.

Apparently bored with looking at my shoes, Judge started checking out the other members of the group. She made note of the fact that one husband wore white socks with dress shoes. She studied the lady with the gray bun and concluded she looked haggard and tired. She stared at the lady across from me working on a quilt. Judge asked me if I thought she gained her weight before or after she got married?

Judge made the rounds, taking mental notes for me. When she came full circle again, she handed me her verdict: *I just don't think you have a whole lot in common with these people. This is more like a group you would bump into in an elevator. Ships passing in the night—that sort of thing. I think you'll be glad when this weekend is over.*

I was thankful no one but me could hear Judge talking. I sent her on her way and tried to focus my attention on the moderator of the group as she spoke.

"I want each of you to think of the kindest thing your spouse has done for you since you've been married. Then if you would like, you can share it with the group."

We were all reflective for a while. The wife of the man wearing white socks spoke first. "Dave has done so many thoughtful things since we've been married. But I guess the most special is when he sent me flowers on my daughter's birthday. All he wrote on the card was: thank you."

The man married to the lady in the gray bun spoke next. "You know, I'm kind of embarrassed. I can think of a hundred things this woman right here beside me has done, but I'm worried that she won't be able to come up with anything for me."

We all laughed.

"I guess that's the nicest thing she's done for me. She's never stopped pouring out her love—even when I don't deserve it."

I waited to hear what the husband of the heavy-set lady would say. He was the last to speak. Reluctantly he began, his voice quivering with nervousness.

Almost instinctively, I wanted to pat him on the shoulder and tell him everything would be all right: he was among friends. His wife had stopped her needlework and looked lovingly at him.

"I guess I have to say," he started again, "that the most loving thing Becky ever did for me was to introduce me to someone who has changed my life. 'George,' she told me one day. 'Jesus is right here beside you, and He wants you to know He loves you.' And you know, I turned around, and there He was."

A tear dripped from Becky's eye and fell onto her quilt. The pattern of her quilt stirred my memory. "Granny's circle" it was called; my grandmother had used the same pattern for her quilts.

As a child, I remember my surprise when I discovered grandmother made our beautiful bed-covers from little bits and pieces of cloth. Differently colored and patterned, she brought them all together in her "granny's circle."

I looked at the people in our little circle of chairs. We were a granny's circle—each of us cut from a different cloth—differently colored and patterned.

Our beauty was not of ourselves but in our relationship to one another. We were all needed in the pattern of that weekend. We passed through a curtain of anonymity and were able to look up into the eyes of each other. We bonded together long enough to laugh and cry as if with one heart.

Somehow I think heaven might come together like that: a granny's circle of humankind.

"What do you think, Judge?"

Three Strikes and Still Batting

"A mistake is evidence that someone has tried to do something."

B.C.

God has a way of making me eat my words.

Before I became a mother, I spent many conversations expounding on what I "would" and "would not" do when I had a child. I verbally raised a lot of children in the twelve years before my daughter arrived!

I remember saying my daughter would not change our life-style that much. "We will still get out and do all the things we've been doing for the past twelve years," I stated matter-of-factly.

That was before I knew a trip to the shopping mall consisted of: a stroller, diapers, bottles, juice, toys, pacifiers, mittens, blankets, a coat, and half a morning to pull it all together. That was before uninterrupted showers and baths disappeared. That was before I realized one had to choose between polished fingernails *or* clean pajamas. That was before I knew baby-sitters got sick, made plans (how dare they?), had homework, or had to be home by ten.

I realized all my comments were premature, dating back to B. C.—before child! I also realized how good my friends were to me: the ones who listened patiently while I shared my B.C. child-rearing philosophies with them; the ones who nodded knowingly as I explained how psychology magically transformed difficult two-year-olds into perfect toddlers; the ones kind enough not to mention all the changes that had occurred in my life-style since my daughter's birth.

And maybe God gave me this spirited little girl so I could grow with her. Some days my brain hurts from trying to use my psychology on her. And instead of hearing: "Yes, Mommy," my days are filled with, "No, Mommy." But I think I'm learning my lesson.

At the store yesterday, I unwrapped a piece of bubble gum (which, of course, I would never allow my child to chew until she was at least five) and stuck it into my two-year-old's mouth. As I did so, I wanted to share with the young woman watching me some of the things I have discovered about child rearing.

But I did not . . . because God has a way of making me eat my words . . . and A. C. advice probably doesn't taste any better than B. C. advice!

The Easter Story

Mandy and I boiled the eggs; she was anxious, so anxious to color her eggs for Easter. She poured the water into the containers and onto the counter. She took the colored tablets and dropped them one by one into each cup of water. Purple, blue, pink, and green streamed from each tablet. She watched, her eyes filled with wonder.

I started to stir the various mixtures to make sure the color tablet had dissolved. "Let me do it," she insisted, grabbing the spoon out of my hand. She stirred each cup vigorously staining my white counter top with pretty pale splashes.

At last, we were ready for the egg dipping. She plopped the first egg into the water so hard it cracked.

"Gently, Honey. You have to be careful; we don't want to crack the egg shells."

Half an hour later, eleven pastel eggs lined the counter.

"Mommy, the Easter bunny comes tomorrow doesn't he?"

"Yes, I believe he does."

"Will he bring me a doll like Santa did at Christmas?" she wanted to know.

"I don't think so. Usually he just brings candy and a few little presents tucked away in an Easter basket."

This was the first Easter she would be old enough to remember. I smiled at the thought of her excitement the next morning. Her Easter basket, the shape of a cute little bunny with big floppy ears, held candy, barrettes, balloons, and a bunny pin. Surely she would be surprised and happy.

As I put away the eggs, my thoughts turned to the reason we celebrate Easter. I silently thanked God for sending His Son so we might find our way home again. I asked Him to help me guide Mandy in her spiritual growth so she, too, would know the joy and peace of faith.

"When she is old enough," I whispered, "I want to tell her what Easter is all about."

Then it occurred to me. Why did I think she was old enough to believe rabbits brought Easter baskets filled with presents and candy, and a fat, jolly man flew in the winter sky with eight reindeer yet I did not think her old enough to understand the Easter story?

A man dying on a cross seemed too cruel a story to tell such an innocent child. But what about Easter morning when Mary came to the garden and saw the stone rolled away? The miracle of resurrection! Surely it would be no harder to explain than how the bunny gets the eggs or why there is a Santa in every shopping mall.

I was reminded of a story a minister told once about a child on Easter morning:

The week before, the minister told the children to bring a gift inside a box that would help tell the Easter story. During the children's sermon, the minister opened the boxes in front of the congregation. One child enclosed a thorn, one a cross, and another a pair of dice. After each gift, the minister explained the meaning of each. Then he opened a box from a little boy who was brain damaged. There was nothing in it. Surprised, the minister looked at the boy. He did not want to embarrass the child, yet he wanted to give him a chance to explain.

"What do we have here?" he asked uneasily.

"An empty tomb," said the boy. Such a profound statement from a boy diagnosed as brain damaged.

I looked over at my little girl. Drops of purple, green, blue, and pink covered her shirt. Who better to believe in the Easter miracle than this small, trusting child?

"Honey, remember I told you about a man named Jesus? Well a long time ago . . ."

The Stain Remover

When the phone rang, I braced myself. Should I answer it? It was nine o'clock. Anita always called around nine o'clock. I had wanted to spend the morning writing. Again and again the ringing shattered the silence, its urgency demanding my attention.

What if Mandy had been injured at school? What if there were an emergency and someone were trying to reach me? What if an editor were calling about my book proposal? The slight chance that it might not be Anita forced me to pick up the receiver.

"Hi," said Anita's familiar voice, "I was afraid you weren't home. But then I remembered you said you were going to try to write some today."

Surely the sound of a voice should not plummet my spirits. But as the hand on my watch marched past 9:30, then 9:45, my morale sank to new depths.

The few words I spoke were delivered in monotone.

"Yes . . . You don't say . . . I see . . . Uhuh."

I tried to say good-bye, but my subtle hint went unnoticed. My resentment deepened. Why didn't she stop to consider my feelings? Didn't she realize I had other things to do with my time?

I struggled with the thought of telling her bluntly how I felt. Would that be charitable of me? Was it worth hurting her feelings and severing our friendship? I decided against honesty.

The town crier, in my head, called "ten o'clock, and time's a wastin'."

I could stand it no longer. In desperation, I took my long cord, walked to the front door, and rang my own doorbell. My heart pounded. Would Anita guess what I had done?

"Is that your doorbell?" she questioned.

"Yes, I guess I had better go answer it. I'll talk to you soon. Bye."

I could not write for the rest of the afternoon. My dishonesty, like a stubborn ink stain, refused to be washed away and forgotten.

"What am I supposed to do, God?" I asked as I stuffed my dirty laundry into the washer. "Why don't I have the courage to be more honest with Anita? What's wrong with saying I only have ten minutes to talk today?"

I picked up my daughter's shirt, stained with spaghetti sauce, and sprayed spot remover on it. I knew the stain would loosen and wash away.

As I held the can of stain remover in my hand, I thought about God's forgiveness. Couldn't He take my conversation with Anita, spray forgiveness on it, and wash it away? Didn't He always remove the ugly stains of my life? Of course, He did!

He, more than anyone, knew the mess I made of things as I bumped my way through life—spilling hurtful words and knocking over good intentions. He, more than anyone, understood my Christian immaturity. He, more than anyone, knew my needs.

If asked, He would launder my soul every night and hand me a clean white robe in the morning. With help, I might someday travel through a day without soiling it.

Perhaps tomorrow . . . if I could muster up enough maturity to suggest to Anita that we shorten our telephone conversations and save our longer chats for lunch.

For the first time in months the thought of answering Anita's phone call the next morning excited me. The honest approach! Not a bad way of dealing with things!

Rose Bowl Bound

A sunny day, two good football teams, and a hot dog—what better way to enjoy a glorious November afternoon? I straightened my shoulders and stood tall for the national anthem. The warm feeling in my chest did not come from the sunshine or my sweater but from being caught up in the noise and hysteria of football. If our team won, they would be going to the Rose Bowl in California on New Year's Day.

Perhaps that explained the electricity of the crowd. People laughed and talked more than usual; excitement traveled from row to row. Strangers talked to strangers because—for a day anyway—we shared something in common. We had only to point to our red jackets and sweaters to confirm it. We were for the red team that readied itself to receive the opening kick.

A hush settled over the crowd as the football arched across the field. Then the crowd came alive when the receiver in the red jersey caught the ball, tucked it under his arm, and began running. Fifteen yards . . . twenty . . . thirty . . . fifty.

People jumped to their feet. Seventy-five yards
. . . eighty-five . . . ninety. Touchdown! A ninety-
five yard touchdown! Pandemonium broke loose.
Confetti snowed down upon us, and signs saying:
"Rose Bowl Bound!" sprinkled the stadium.

The signs weaved and bobbed in a sea of bodies, bodies that came together for one reason—to
cheer for a team. How odd it was really—thousands of seats surrounding a patch of ground
marked with yellow and white lines; men running
around like ants, a ball being carried back and
forth between two posts, and people becoming
entrapped in the frenzy of losing or winning—all
depending on where the ants ran.

In the scheme of things, where did it fit in? Five
years from now, next year, after football season,
who would remember or even care about the
events unfolding on the field? Thousands of people gathered every week across the nation to
watch twenty-two people pursue a ball made from
animal hide.

Suddenly, I felt like shouting: "This is mad-
ness! How can we keep from laughing at ourselves? Look up. The sky above us never ends.
Doesn't that leave you in awe? Look at our bodies.
Aren't they miraculous? Look at this stadium
filled with ninety thousand people. Not one of us
is alike. Isn't that incredible? And, yet we all have
something in common—we possess this thing
called life. Doesn't that astound you?"

The crowd stood and cheered. Our team had
scored another touchdown, but for a moment I

imagined that we cheered for something more than a player running toward a metal goal. I pictured us rising to honor the greatest Man in all history. One who suited up in human flesh and stepped down onto earth. And I imagined that, when he walked out onto the field, ninety thousand voices stilled and ninety thousand hearts stirred . . .

Why can't it be true? Instead of applauding football teams, why can't we applaud the Son of God every week? I don't know the answer. I only know that I keep going to football games. But I do have a prayer. I wrote it one night . . . before the big game.

A Football Fan's Prayer

Lord, please help me get my priorities straight.
I know You do not mind if I go to a football game.
But help me be as anxious to fill a seat in the pew
    as I am the one in the stadium.
Let me sing more praises than fight songs.
Help me look up at least as often as I look down-
    field.
Help me applaud You more loudly than I ap-
    plaud man.
And finally . . .
Help me to wear Your team colors with more
    pride and honor than I have wearing those
    of my football team.

                                        Amen.

Laughter
Is Not Always the Best Medicine

I used to wonder what harm could come from a few wise cracks. What was wrong with poking fun at the "weird" lady in the elevator, in the privacy of my friends' company? It wasn't every day I saw someone wearing only one earring and one eyebrow. (Punk rock had not emerged yet.)

What was wrong with cracking a joke to my sister about the lady at the bus stop wearing a bright floral dress, a hat, and "would you believe it: tennis shoes and bobby socks?"

Why should my friend's feelings be hurt because I pinched my nose shut while I passed around her hot hors d'oeuvres: What did she expect when she served broiled oysters on crackers?

Or what about the neighbor lady who planted flowers in the oddest fashion—one petunia, one sunflower, one begonia, one geranium—all in a circle? Most of the neighbors saw the humor in the comment, "Why don't you let Mrs. Johnson help you plant your flowers this year?"

Of course, none of us would have ever said anything to Mrs. Johnson. It was not our intention to hurt her; we only thought her curious and funny.

But another experience with my youngest sister jarred me into realizing that laughter should not be at the expense of someone else.

"Now that is what I call an outfit," I said to my sister as I pointed to the little old lady at the bus stop. "Tennis shoes, bobby socks, and a hat. Remind me to look for that one in the designer section."

My sister's head whirled toward me. Her look of disbelief was not over the fact that an old lady wore tennis shoes with her dress and hat. No. She could not believe that her oldest sister, the one she so admired, would make fun of an old woman and most probably a poor one. The look I saw in her eyes said things to me I did not want to hear about myself, things I would not soon forget.

She made me wonder about the woman in the elevator with one earring and one eyebrow? Who was I to judge her? What if she were emotionally disturbed or sadly addicted to drugs? Should laughter be my reaction to her? Should I remember to tell my friends all about her? Or should I remember to pray for her instead?

And my friend who served oysters on crackers? Should I, her closest friend, who knew cooking to be her Achilles' heel, use the situation just to get a laugh?

And Mrs. Johnson who bent over her flowers, planting them tenderly? Was a circle of fluffy impatiens any more pleasing to God than her circle of color and variety? Did God care that her flower garden did not quite fit into the neighborhood "norm" for flower gardens?

No. I had a feeling God might have liked hers best.

Even though my outfits matched and my flowers brought a compliment or two, on the inside I must have looked like a veritable clown to God.

How laughable I must have been with one eyebrow wrinkled in judgment, a pair of tennis shoes clashing with my crooked, self-hung halo, and a heart full of dandelions and thistles.

And yet I heard no laughter coming from heaven, no wise cracks: I felt only the loving arms of my Father as He tried to teach me compassion.

The Return

I left the wallpaper store trying to decide if the bathroom really needed to be wallpapered. The paper cost more than I thought it would, but that soft coral print was so pretty. I just could not make up my mind.

On my way to the car, I remembered I needed to get two boxes of plastic sheets for my files. Some people cannot resist bakeries or candy shops. I cannot resist the lure of an office supply or stationery store.

I fingered the notebooks, flipped through the files, and checked the prices on the big boxes of envelopes. When I got to the cash register, my arms held much more than the two boxes of plastic sheets I had come in for. There were paper clips, a new file basket, a big roll of labels, a flip file for my addresses, pencils, and some typing paper.

When the clerk rang up the bill, I thought it sounded a bit low, but I paid him what he asked and took my bag to the car. There I opened it and compared my purchases with the cash register receipt. Just as I suspected. The clerk had undercharged me; he had only rung up one box of plastic sheets instead of two.

What a deal! The sheets cost eleven dollars a box. I got two for the price of one.

I drove home feeling good about the error made in my favor. Of course, had the error been to my disadvantage, I would have gone back. But after rationalizing the situation, I figured there were plenty of times I had been shortchanged at the grocery or department stores and probably never even noticed.

It all works out in the end, I told myself.

As I put away the things in my office, I came upon a story I had just mailed to the editor of a Sunday School magazine. A nagging feeling pulled at me. I wrote about God, love, truth, and kindness.

What had I done one hour earlier? Rubbed my greedy hands together and delighted in the fact I had received something for nothing!

I knew I would have to make amends. The store had already closed. But the next morning, as soon as the store opened, I handed my receipt to the clerk.

"Hi. I came in here yesterday and bought two boxes of your plastic sheets for ringed binders."

"Yes?"

"Well, you only charged me for one box."

"Excuse me?" he said incredulously.

I was sure he heard what I said, but I repeated it just the same.

"Yesterday, I bought two boxes of these plastic sheets, and you only charged me for one."

He shook his head. "Just a minute, I need to go talk to the manager."

I overheard him saying something about "a lady who says we undercharged her."

The manager eyed me carefully. They continued to talk, then the clerk came back.

"Well, I guess you owe us eleven dollars then. Thank you for coming back. It is a little unusual though."

I did not want to bask too long in his praise or tell him of my initial reaction. I paid the eleven dollars and went outside feeling much happier.

I was so happy, in fact, that I decided to go next door to the wallpaper store and buy that wallpaper for the bathroom. When I told the lady what I wanted, she said, "Well, today must be your lucky day! We just reduced that paper this morning. It's 30 percent off!"

Just a Little Something

Before Christmas, my husband and I walked our daughter Mandy through countless toy stores, narrowing her choices to three favorite gifts. Those would be from "Santa." She repeatedly pointed to baby dolls with little blue eyes that closed whenever you laid them down. And then she wanted winter boots for building snowmen and an over-sized block set. We agreed those were good choices, so we smuggled them into the house one night after bedtime.

My Christmas shopping was done. Or so I thought, until I saw a small pink Bible on the sale table at the bookstore. I recalled a conversation with Mandy one morning before Sunday school. "Can I take a Bible too?" she had wanted to know.

"Honey, you don't have a Bible," I answered. "But you can take this booklet and pretend it's a Bible."

That appeased her and each week thereafter she took her pretend Bible to church. She was only three, but I decided to buy her the Bible. It looked like it would rest perfectly in the palm of

her hand. And it was just a little something—
certainly not as big and expensive as her other
gifts. I took it home, wrapped it in tissue paper,
and placed it in the bough of the tree.

On Christmas Eve Jim and I decided that
Mandy could open one gift—a little present to
hold her over until Christmas day. We did not
want to "spoil" the really big surprises, so I
reached into the tree bough and presented my
daughter with the small package wrapped in tissue paper.

She unwrapped it and smiled.

"Now you have your very own Bible," I exulted.

"Oh, Mommy and Daddy, thank you. That was
so sweet of you. How did you know that is just
what I wanted?" They were grown-up words spoken from a child's heart.

She stroked the leather binding and flipped
through pages that she could not yet read. I read
her the inscription: "To Mandy, the greatest
blessing God has ever given us. Love, Mommy &
Daddy." She hugged our necks and insisted on
taking the Bible with her to church that night—
and then to her aunt and uncle's.

Several days after Christmas when Mandy's
baby doll had been christened "Trisha" and her
blocks had been turned into Cinderella's castle
and her snow boots had their first trial run outside
to feed the birds, I asked her what was her favorite
Christmas present. She put her small finger to her
cheek and thought for a moment.

"I think," she mused, "that I like my Bible best."

Her answer surprised me. I had bought the Bible, certainly, but not because I thought it would be her favorite gift. I gave it to her on Christmas Eve as a little token of the "great expectations" of Christmas morning. Amazing how God can use my imperfect reasoning and turn it into beauty and truth.

Because, after all, the Bible is a token of "great expectations" to come.

The Gift

My daughter lay sleeping behind pulled shades. Rarely did she ever fall asleep in the middle of the afternoon. Her energetic body seemed able to run full speed from daylight to darkness without rest. But today . . . ah today . . . she slept.

How I wanted to fix myself a glass of iced tea, brush the dust from the cover of Anne Morrow Lindbergh's *Gift from the Sea* and go outside and read in my glider.

How I wanted Lindbergh's philosophical words to soothe me again. The memory of her words had faded in my mind. What was it she said about loving and life that had made my step lighter and my love shinier? The winter had been a long one. My spirit wanted to burst forth like the dogwood blossoms, but I had forgotten how to bloom.

Besides there were too many things waiting to be done—sewing, ironing, paper work—things that took twice as long when two chubby little hands tried "to help." So a free afternoon was too valuable to waste doing nothing. I pulled my list of "things to do" from the shelf.

I did not see the loose light bulb on top of the pad. What I did see was an explosion of glass when it hit the floor. One small light bulb shattered into a thousand pieces. Evidently, my husband had put it on top of my list, so I would not forget to special order two of them for him.

I looked around in disbelief. How could one light bulb break into so many pieces? Tiny slivers of glass covered the floor, my desk, the table, and some even found their way to the toy basket on the other side of the room.

I swept up glass and brushed away tears. What a waste of time! I had so many better things to do than clean up a mess that could have been avoided. I was mad—at my husband, at myself, and at life in general.

By the time I finished sweeping, mopping, and wiping, I was sure Mandy would be rousing any minute. Rather than start a project, I poured myself a glass of iced tea, took my book, and seated myself comfortably in the glider. If Mandy wakened, I would be able to hear her from the open window above me.

The broken light bulb had given birth to a pessimist: "You better not get too comfortable," she said. "This won't last long."

But the sun wrapped its warm arms around me, and I could not help but respond. The pages of my book flapped in the wind, my mind traveled on the words of truth, and the world let me slip from its fingers. I did not know if only one hour passed or two. I did not even care. I lay lost in an amber afternoon of solitude, the very solitude Lindbergh mentioned in her book.

"For it is not physical solitude that actually separates one from other men," she wrote. "Not physical isolation, but spiritual isolation. It is not the desert island nor the stony wilderness that cuts you from the people you love. . . . If one is out of touch with oneself, then one cannot touch others . . . for me, the core, the inner spring, can best be refound through solitude."[1]

I looked up at the sky and the clouds sailing past. I had found my core, my inner spring. The gift of solitude had been given to me, and I knew from whom it had come. It had come from the One who hears my prayers, from the One who knows when my spirit withers and needs watered, from the One who makes my wide-eyed daughter sleep for three hours in the middle of the afternoon.

My gift had come from God, who sometimes uses broken light bulbs . . . to help a heart shine brighter.

1. Anne Morrow Lindbergh, *Gift from the Sea* (New York: Walker & Co., 1985), p. 44.

Where Do I Go from Here, Lord?

"If there is no way out, there is always a way up!"

The Clink of Armor

It seemed like every magazine I opened contained an article about the importance of morning devotion. *Guideposts, Reader's Digest, The Christian Writer,* and even a pamphlet, *My Personal Prayer Diary* written by Catherine Marshall and Leonard LeSourd.

Usually, I consider the "recurring coincidences" in my life as spiritual lessons. If something comes to my attention three or four times, I believe it is for a reason. But rousing me from my warm sheets an hour earlier in the morning was no easy task—no matter how powerfully and positively the authors relayed their morning devotional experiences.

"One hour that can change your life" promised an article in *Reader's Digest.*

Catherine Marshall wrote about a way to prepare for the difficult days in which we live. To her, the best way to deal with the attack on morals, religious beliefs, and standards of decency was to suit up in God's armor.

"How can we put on the armor unless we are

knowledgeable about the equipment provided us.
. . . Daily food in absorbing the Word of God is
just as much needed as food for our bodies," she
said. "Daily communication face-to-face with the
One who can help us and rescue us is indispens-
able."[1]

Writer-mother-homemaker Marlene Bagnull
came to the same conclusion in an article in *The
Christian Writer*. She said that juggling her
schedule so that none of her jobs were neglected
seemed an impossibility. But she discovered the
more she had to do, the more she needed to
pray.[2]

Homer Figler also lauded the benefits of morning devotional time in *Guideposts*. He wrote that
the more he continued his daily reading, the more
"helpful messages" kept coming to him. "It was
almost uncanny the way they would relate to
something facing me on a particular day."[3]

I did not doubt what these people said. I only
doubted that I would feel better waking up earlier. I almost always prayed at night before I went
to bed. Sure, I went to sleep sometimes in the
middle of my prayers or got sidetracked occasionally, but God and I had special times together.

I decided to pray about it one night. "If you
want me to start having a morning devotion time
with You, Lord, just let me know."

The next morning I woke up an hour earlier
than usual and could not go back to sleep. "OK,"
I said as I reached for my Bible. "I give up."

The stillness of early morning lay unbroken in

the sitting room. I read my Bible without interruption. I prayed for everyone who came to mind. I pictured my daughter and husband surrounded in the warm healing light of God's love. I poured out my concerns and fears, my dreams and my hurts. And then I asked God to be with me as I went through my day.

Suddenly, Catherine Marshall's words about God's armor became clear. Morning devotion would give me a chance to put on that armor. I could dress myself in His Word and ask Him to guide and protect me instead of coming to Him at night seeking first aid.

Was it my imagination or did the days seem to flow smoother after that discovery? Was it my imagination, or did I feel like I had an extra hour of rest? Was it my imagination, or did it seem easier to smile at the lady who honked impatiently behind me because the light blinked green two seconds earlier?

Was it my imagination, or did I actually hear the faint clink of armor . . . in the early hours of morning?

1. Catherin Marshall and Leonard LeSourd, *My Personal Prayer Diary* (Old Tappan, N.J.: Chosen Books, 1979) exerpted in *Guideposts*, "My 30-Day Prayer Diary," p. 3.

2. Marlene Bagnull, "First Things First," *The Christian Writer*, April 1984, p. 30.

3. Homer Figler, "My Minister Meant Business," *Guideposts*, April 1984, p. 36.

I Love You . . . But

"I love you," I told my husband, Jim, "but you never send me flowers anymore or take me on picnics."

"I love you . . . but you watch too much television."

"I love you . . . but you eat too fast."

"I love you . . . but."

"Nag, nag, nag," he might have said. Or he might have answered, "You sure have a funny way of showing it." But more often than not, he ate slower, promised to ease up on the television, and located a romantic spot for a picnic.

It was not until after some earnest praying that I began to see that much of the love I gave to Jim was conditional. I would love him *if* he loved me. I would love him *if* he treated me kindly. I would love him *if* he acted in a manner that was pleasing to me.

Dr. Ed Wheat's book *Love Life* helped me yearn for a different kind of love—*agapē* love: the kind of love that heals all the woundings of marriage; the kind of love that leaps walls where human love stops cold; the kind of love that does not need to be fed, yet it feeds.

Dr. Wheat wrote, "To the relationship of husband and wife, which would otherwise lie at the mercy of fluctuating emotions and human upheavals, agape imparts stability and a permanence that is rooted in the Eternal. Agape is the Divine solution for marriages populated by imperfect human beings!"[1]

How well Paul knew this. He wrote to the Corinthians about a love free of conditions. I had read Paul's message many times, but one night the words pulled tears from my eyes.

"Love is very patient and kind, never jealous or envious, never boastful or proud, never haughty or selfish or rude. Love does not demand its own way. It is not irritable or touchy. It does not hold grudges and will hardly even notice when others do it wrong" (1 Cor. 13:4-5).

I lay in bed thinking upon these words. And as I lay there, I moved my hand to Jim's side of the bed. I touched his chest that rose and fell in the rhythm of sleep. I snuggled against his warmth.

How lonely my life would be without him. How patient he was to listen to my attempts to define life and loving and God and man and all the other countless question marks that overtake my thinking and conversations. How sweet that in sixteen years of marriage he had never once walked out the door of a morning without kissing me goodbye. How sad that many times my words and actions did not reveal the soft, tender feelings within me.

"Why is it, God, that I struggle so to love as You love? What is there inside me that finds it almost impossible not to notice if I have been wronged? What do I have to do in order to love unconditionally? You know I love Jim, but sometimes . . ."

A gentle thought floated into my mind: *Don't love Jim, but . . . love him even though . . .*

1. Ed Wheat, M.D., *Love Life* (Grand Rapids: Zondervan, 1980), p. 119.

Overcoming My Handicap

"What do I say to a blind lady, Lord? Please help me to say and do the right things."

I took a deep breath and rang her doorbell.

"Well, hi, Terry," she said in a chipper voice. "Did you have any trouble finding my house?"

"No, your directions were perfect, Helen."

She felt for the lock and closed the door.

"Now if I can just hold onto your arm, here, I'll be able to walk beside you just fine."

She placed her arm inside of mine, and I led her down the steps toward the car.

"You know," she said, "I'm just so glad we're finally able to meet each other in person. I just knew from the first time I called you that we were going to become friends. I don't have too many friends who share my love for writing," she confided.

Her small feet kept step with mine and met the steps with grace and certainty. No doubt after living in her house for forty years, she saw them clearly in her mind.

She gave me directions to a Chinese restaurant she had chosen.

"You can park right by the front door in the handicapped space," she said as she handed me a special tag to hang on my rearview mirror. "Isn't that a handy thing?" she laughed.

I guided her into the door of the restaurant. She told the host there would be two for lunch, and he seated us at a table near the window.

"Now, if you will do the honors and read today's specials, I would appreciate it," she said, putting me totally at ease.

We ended up with pepper steak and chicken chow mein.

"Now tell me about your writing," she insisted. "Have you been able to do much since you moved here? Where have you published?"

The time slipped away as we talked about our love for the written word. Only Helen's written words were braille. She told me about her special typewriter, her autobiography that had just been published, and her former job as a braille proofreader for the publishing house of the blind. She was now retired.

As I led her back to her front door, I realized what a special lady she was. Her ready smile, her good-natured disposition, and her faith were all the qualities I so admired in a person. I knew we would become very good friends.

"Thank you for treating me to lunch," I said, as I waved good-bye.

I smiled. I had forgotten. Helen could not see

me waving. Then it occurred to me how beautifully God had answered my panicky flash prayer.

"What do you say to a blind lady?" I had asked.

"The same things you say to a sighted one," He
had answered.

A Verse Meant Just for Me

One night I lay on my bed feeling lonely and depressed. My husband was out of town, and my daughter slept in her bed. The quietness of the house settled on the pillows around me. No crisis could account for my feelings. I was, in fact, just weary. My prayers the past few days were barren and dry. I was filled with doubts.

I wrote about helping others, but I began to wonder if God wanted me to do more? Instead of pushing buttons on a keyboard, did He want me to walk the streets until I found shelter for the city's homeless? Did He want me to do more than send a check to feed the world's starving population? Did He consider my writing a valid ministry? What's more, did I?

What was it I once read on a poster? "The smallest deed is worth more than the biggest intention." After all, it was much easier to "write about" than "right" the injustices of the world.

Like a small child, I curled up under my covers seeking comfort. I opened my Bible, and my eyes fell on Philippians 2:13. "For God is at work within you, helping you want to obey him, and then helping you do what he wants."

What relief I felt! If I earnestly sought to do God's work, then according to that Scripture, God would lead me in the right direction. Fretting and worrying would not help. In fact they were counterproductive. Fulton Sheen went so far as to say, "Worry is a form of atheism."

How true.

If I did not expect God to give me directions after I had asked, if I did not trust that His hand rested upon my life, then what good were my prayers?

I read the Bible verse again. "For God is at work within you, helping you want to obey him, and then helping you do what he wants."

Tears sprang to my eyes. How beautifully God works. That was not the first time an answer had come when I opened my Bible at random. Nor, I knew, would it be the last.

The skeptic might wrinkle his brow and say, "Surely you don't really believe God answers prayers that way?"

Then I would admit, "Yes, I do. I truly do. Maybe some night, when you ache to hear God speak . . . maybe you, too, can open your Bible . . . and read a verse meant just for you!"

Material Manifestation: 1A

What if, I asked myself. *What if I chose the life I now find myself in?*

That type of question comes to me when I find myself flying thirty-five thousand feet above the earth. Looking down at houses and bridges that can fit into the palm of my hand changes my perspective. I know under each tiny roof there are problems—some problems are so big that they are destroying the very souls that struggle under the weight of them.

But somehow, from where I sat in the DC-10, it seemed to me that problems were meant to strengthen instead of pulverize.

I let my imagination fly . . .

What if God were talking to two souls before they were born?

"Life will not be easy as a human," God tells them. "You will forget what you know now. You will be changed into helpless infants, struggle with material limitations, and, hardest of all, you will encounter trials and tribulations which will

threaten to destroy the very faith you seek to puri-
fy."

Do you really think that's possible? I asked myself.

I don't know, said the truth seeker within me. *But
just suppose these two souls were adamant. Suppose they
wanted very much to prove their love for God by taking
the test of becoming human. The course required to pass
this test was: Material Manifestation: 1A. Suppose God
granted their wish and sent them to earth.*

Once on earth, they both forgot all they had
known before. Human joy and sorrow filled them.
They came to know the miracle of birth. And, at
first, neither one thought much about God.

Then, gradually, one of the souls felt a stirring
within him. He felt a yearning when he looked at
the night sky. He began to remember, not con-
sciously, but unconsciously.

His faith deepened. Not because of what he
could "prove" but because of what he felt to be
true. And he gave all he had. When he died, there
was great rejoicing among the angels.

But the other soul struggled with her problems.
She found herself a victim of the material world.
And the farther away she got from the truth, the
more desperate she became. She searched for
comfort and love in the material realm: beautiful
clothes, prestigious awards, and treasures from
every corner of the world.

But somehow the hollowness of life never filled
her. She had little to share with those around her
because she had little left inside her. Somewhere
in the test of life, she had lost herself. It wasn't

until she died that she remembered why she had come. And the pain that remembering brought her was unbearable; her tears fell on the loving arms of her Father.

"Why," she implored, "why couldn't I remember?"

From the plane window, I looked out into the vastness of the horizon.

Please, God. Please don't let me flunk Material Manifestation: 1A.

One
One-Thousandth of a Second

I had just finished reading Madeleine L'Engel's book *Walking on Water*. My own feet splashed in the sea water.

Vacation! How wonderful to sit beneath a palm tree and read a book. How wonderful to walk at my leisure on the glistening sand and not have to worry about dirty dishes, ringing telephones, and a voice in the night calling, "Mommy." I felt as if a sign dangled from my neck: "Closed. Off duty in an island paradise."

The act of "being," a skill I had almost lost touch with, rekindled itself within me. And as a sea gull squawked overhead, I felt myself floating in the cloudless sky beside him—wings spread in the wind, floating in blue space.

Then I became a sea shell tumbling in the churning foam at my feet. I felt myself mixing with cool saltiness. Buoyed by a strength and power beyond myself, I was set free.

My breathing sounded to the rhythm of the waves. My sighs caught upon the wind, and my heart danced to the music of life. Happiness flooded my every atom. My consciousness thrust itself into a new dimension. A place where all thoughts were things and a place where all things were possible.

In her book, Madeleine L'Engle said that we humans have forgotten much since time began. We have forgotten how to walk on water, speak to the angels, and move, unfettered, among the stars. Like Peter, we occasionally step out in faith and almost succeed in doing the impossible. But then we look around, doubt fills us, and we sink once again into our modern, scientific probabilities.

I looked out upon the water. What were Peter's thoughts as Jesus held out His hand to him? Was Peter filled with doubts and fears? Did he want to laugh? To cry? Whatever Peter felt, he stepped from the boat—perhaps into the dimension where all things are possible—and walked upon water.

The impossible became possible.

I smiled at the absurdity of my next move. I raised my foot and stepped confidently onto the ocean. Was it my imagination, or did I, for one one thousandth of a second, feel the firm smoothness of solid water like cold marble beneath my foot? Did I, for one one thousandth of a second, become suspended above the sand?

Not one head turned on shore. After all, what was so unusual about a woman wading in the ocean? Nothing, I guess. Except that . . . maybe . . . for one one thousandth of a second, she had become all that she was capable of being.

Beyond Reflections

I returned to the river where my sisters and I rode the rapids without the benefit of boats or inner tubes. The same Texas sun that had tanned our gangly arms and legs a deep, golden brown by summer's end burned overhead. The echoes of our laughter escaped from the past to mix with the sound of rushing water.

We used to jump into that bubbling, churning washing-machine river. Our heads bobbed in and out of the rapids. The sixty-second ride thrilled us. It was a fast and seemingly reckless ride. It sucked the breath out of me, and I repeated the experience time and time again until I became too exhausted to keep my head above water. Afterward, I pulled myself out of the water and hugged the big flat rock. It warmed me while I dried.

I looked for the rock again. Then I saw it—downstream; its face unchanged by the same years that had so changed me. I climbed onto its warm, smooth surface. A familiar feeling settled about me. According to the calendar, twenty-five years had passed; but it seemed like my hair had barely had time to dry.

I dangled my feet in the cool water. Clouds, trees, and sunshine floated in the reflection. Below the reflection, a lazy fish swam slowly away.

Tiny silver minnows, like slivers of sunlight, darted between the rocks; a water spider carried a bubble of air to his nest; and long, mosslike fingers rippled in the current. Another world existed right below my feet—a world I had splashed in, sat beside, and looked at but never seen until that moment.

That revelation made me question what else I had blindly stumbled by in my lifetime. What other worlds waited to be discovered?

Christ's words came to my mind. "The kingdom of God is within you."

Since that is true, how many times have I splashed in it, sat beside it, looked at it, but never really seen it? How many times have I been carried on the rapids of life and never paused to look below the surface? How many times have I brushed against a pair of feet nailed to a cross . . . and never once looked up?

An All-purpose Prayer

Some of us are searching
For the right word,
Like the Centurion who asked: "Lord,
Only say the word, and
My servant shall be healed."
Others are lost and
Need only a gesture from you
As Philip did:
"Lord, show us the way."
Some of us are still struggling
With prehistoric monsters
Like resentment. And we
Bite our lips because
We have to go back and ask you once more
So dumb a question as Peter
Blurted out: "Lord,
How often can my brother offend me,
And I still forgive him?"
Finally, there are those beside us
Who do not have the heart
For any more questions.
They don't even know what to ask
And pray blindly

Through their tears
Simply for you to sit beside them
As you did John that night.
And if there is anyone
Who could not bear that much light
Would you please nod to them, or
Glance their way, or remember them,
Lord, as you promised you would the thief,
"When you come into your Kingdom"?

—From *Before You Call I Will Answer* by David A. Redding copyright ©
1985 by David A. Redding. Published by Fleming H. Revell Company.
Used by permission.

Epilogue

As I come to the end of this book, I realize I may have made the biggest goof of all—thinking that what I have to say is of some importance. Daring to think that maybe my words might change your outlook or bring your walk closer to God. That is my desire. Oh, I will be pleased to see my book in print; certainly, that weakness in my character will puff with pride.

But the other part of me, the part that is humble and noble, that part of me that is as fleeting as a falling star, that part of me hopes I have given you a glimpse of the love and forgiveness that is ours for the asking. Deep down, beyond pride and human emotions, I hope I have taken you by the hand and shared with you the times I, too, have told half-truths, said unkind words, and been blinded by circumstances. It is at those times that I have needed God's presence.

I have made many other mistakes in my life, monumental mistakes, mistakes that have hurt others very deeply, mistakes that were so painful I do not have the strength to expose them. But

God has seen me through them. He has taken all the broken pieces and my impure motives and turned them into something beautiful. He has used them to teach me valuable lessons. He has blessed me with forgiveness. And He promises to do the same for every child of His.

There is one thought I would like to leave with you. I do not know if it is an original thought or one that has meant so much to me that I have adopted it. Whatever the case, I hope you will adopt it, too . . .

Always remember that God loves you so much that He sees you *not as you are, but for what you strive to be.*

For that, my friend, is the key to forgiveness!